Air Fryer Cookbook UK 2021

Quick and Delicious Recipes for the Whole Year incl. Desserts and Side Dishes

Amber C. Gardner

ISBN- 9798592220654

TABLE OF CONTENTS

INTRODUCTION

If you've been given an air fryer as a gift and you're not sure what to do with it, or you're considering purchasing one, this book is your one-stop guide to everything air fryer-related!

Packed with information and hints and tips on how to use your air fryer, it's also crammed to the hilt with delicious recipes to try.

This book will show you just how versatile your air fryer is, showing you how to cook a variety of different meals with a wide range of ingredients. From different meats to vegetables, appetisers to desserts, your new household gadget can do all of it, in the healthiest and cleanest of ways.

First things first however, what exactly is an air fryer, and what does it do?

What is an Air Fryer?

An air fryer is an appliance which cooks your food, to give it the simplest explanation. It is far more advanced than that however, as it cooks food using hot air, rather than oil. You will all be very familiar with the regular deep fat fryer, which uses an abundance of hot oil to heat up and cook your food, leaving you with crispy, albeit extremely unhealthy meals and snacks as a result.

Now, an air fryer still gives you the fried crisp you want, but it does it by using air rather than oil, and therefore avoiding that saturated fat, artery clogging effect that a deep fat fryer has. The air is circulated around the machine by a convection technique, which is extremely complicated, but does the job very well! A fan inside the fryer pushes the air deep into the machine, so none of your ingredients are missed, giving you delicious, crispy food in a fraction of time.

The end result is home cooked meals which are cost effective as a result, healthy, lacking in dripping oil, and also super easy to use too. An air fryer is completely suitable for a first timer or a total cooking beginner. Most of the time you simply place your ingredients into the fryer and allow the machine to do its thing!

From our second chapter onwards we will be exploring the various different meals and snacks you can make using an air fryer, and that will show just how versatile and varied this machine can be. Before that however, we need to delve a little further into the wonderful world of the air fryer, to complete your basic knowledge.

AIR FRYER 101

You'll probably be ready and raring to go, eager to start making delicious meals in your new air fryer, or maybe you're ready to head out and buy one right now! Whatever your starting point, we need to learn a little more about this useful piece of kitchen kit, before we get ready to set sail on a journey into delicious and easy to make recipes.

An air fryer works, as we have mentioned earlier, by pushing hot air around the inner pot, therefore cooking your food to a crisp. The ingredients are placed into a basket, much like a deep fat fryer, and then lowered into the main cooking chamber, with the lid closed. The heating mechanism then creates the extreme heat, which is pushed around the pot by a fan. This fast movement of air crisps your food, without using oil to do the job for you.

Benefits of Using an Air Fryer

You might wonder why you should bother purchasing an air fryer when you can simply use your old deep fat fryer instead. The bottom line comes down to health, and there is nothing more important than that!

The benefits of choosing to use an air fryer are:

- ➳ Cook your food quickly and easily

- Easy for beginners to use

- Far healthier than deep fat frying

- Gives you crispy food, without the unhealthy element of oil

- Ideal if you have children who love the crispy fried foods that are terrible for your health, because you can recreate the same effect with far less calories and fat using an air fryer

- Most air fryer parts are suitable to be cleaned in the dishwasher, although do check the instructions of your particular model

- Easy to clean, thanks to no added oils or fats

- Frozen food is cooked to a crisp quickly and easily, or you can cook from scratch

- Your kitchen won't become overheated when using an air fryer, like it would with a deep fat fryer

- It is a cost-effective investment which will allow you to make a huge number of different meals and snacks with ease

Things to Consider When Purchasing an Air Fryer

By this point you've probably decided that an air fryer is for you, but there are a few things you need to bear in mind when making your purchase, if you haven't already.

There are a few things you cannot make in an air fryer, such as anything which has a liquid-style batter. This will simply not cook properly and will make a mess of your machine! You can however freeze your batters first and then add them to the machine, which would do the same thing in effect. You should also realise that if you're cooking for a large group of people, you're probably going to need to do a few batches of food, as most air fryers do not have a large capacity.

Slight disadvantages to one side, what do you really need to look for/ consider when making your purchase?

- **Price** - Air fryers can be expensive if you go for the top of the range choices. Shop around and find a product which suits your price needs. Larger capacity and more features usually points to a higher price tag, so this is something to think about before making a decision.

- **How much space do you have?** - Most air fryers are quite large, even if the inner capacity isn't that much. This is because of the fan and the heating mechanism inside, so make sure that you have enough space on your kitchen work surface, or in a cupboard.

- **Features** - If you've never used an air fryer before, it's probably not going to be the case that you need an all singing, all dancing machine. Check out the various features on different models and go with an option you feel comfortable with.

- **Brand name and guarantee** - If you want peace of mind, opt for a big brand name, which will usually come with a sizeable guarantee. This is a vital piece of the puzzle if you're making a medium to large cost investment.

Air Fryer Maintenance

Looking after your air fryer properly will mean that it lasts much longer as a result. So, what do you need to know about maintaining your air fryer properly? It's basically about cleaning it well and cleaning it often. The bad news? It's best to clean it after every use, but the good news is that it's not difficult to clean, and most air fryers have certain parts which you can simply take out and place in the dishwasher; again, do be sure to check with your particular instruction manual to be sure yours falls into that category.

Avoid using anything abrasive on the inside of your fryer as the coating can easily be scratched away, so avoid anything metal, steel wool or sponges with a rough edge. It's also best to never completely submerge your air fryer in water. Remember, the main part of your fryer is electric!

Follow these instructions to effectively clean your air fryer:

- Turn off and unplug your air fryer and let it cool down

- Remove the basket and the pan

- Use a damp cotton cloth with wipe the outside of the main unit

- Use warm water and a sponge (remember, non-abrasive) to wipe the inside of the main unit, being sure to get rid of any crispy pieces that have stuck to the inner wall

- Turn the fryer upside down and wipe the heating section of the appliance

- Check instructions, bust most baskets and pans are safe to be placed in the dishwasher. If not, you can wash these with hot water and a soft sponge, but make sure that any crispy residue is removed

- Allow everything to air dry

- Reassemble your air fryer

If you find that your air fryer begins to smell a little over time, which may happen even with careful cleaning, you could place half a lemon inside the main basket and pan and allow it to sit there for around half an hour. Afterwards clean as normal and allow to air dry. This should get rid of any nasty niffs!

AIR FRYER TROUBLESHOOTING

There are a few common issues which can arise with air fryers, but the good news is that they can usually be fixed yourself, without any major problems. Let's look at a few of the most common issues and how to solve them.

Dry/Chewy or Even Soggy Food

Remember that you are not using oil, so sometimes food may basically be baked rather than fried. The best way to avoid this is to actually use a very small amount of oil just to coat the food very slightly. This will give you the extra crispiness you need, if you are having this problem. Having said that, high quality air fryers should not give you this issue.

White Smoke

Black smoke is a problem and needs to be seen by a technician, however white smoke is something you can easily rectify at home. This basically means that there is a high amount of fat contained within the food you're trying to cook. White smoke isn't harmful, but it is annoying, so simply make sure that the oil collection part of the machine is clean and empty it on a regular basis.

No Power

If you're trying to turn on your air fryer and nothing is happening, then check that everything is properly connected before you panic, make sure the wires are attached to the right place, e.g. power cable, and obviously make sure it is turned on! You might also want to check the fuse inside the plug. Check the timer and see if it's simply a case of not setting it; some fryers need you to set the timer before the power will kick in. If you've tried all of this and nothing seems to be rectifying the problem, return your fryer and get it changed/fixed.

Tips For Using Your New Air Fryer

We're almost at the most exciting part - the recipes! Before we get onto that however, let's give you a few final handy tips for use when you finally purchase and begin to cook with your new air fryer.

- Preheat your air fryer for a few minutes before you place your food inside

- Coat your food with oil (slightly) if it doesn't already have an oily film on the outside. For instance, meat is already slightly oily so won't need extra but vegetables and battered items will

- Great the bottom of your basket so that your food doesn't stick

- Make sure that you don't place too much food inside the basket. If you do this, the food won't cook well. It is best to cook in batches in this case

- If you're cooking wings or fries, make sure you give them a shake whilst you're cooking them; every few minutes should be enough

- If you want the best outcome in terms of crispiness, spray your food with a small amount of oil at the halfway cooking point

- Don't simply use the hottest temperature to get crispiness, adjust your temperature for certain foods

Now it's time to get to the good part - the recipes!

Air Fryer Breakfast Recipes

Potato Hash, Sweet Style

Serves - 6
Calories - 191, protein - 3.7g, fat - 6g, carbs - 31.4g

INGREDIENTS:

- 2 sweet potatoes, cubed
- 2 slices of bacon, cut into small cubes
- 2 tbsp olive oil
- 1 tbsp smoked paprika
- 1 tsp salt
- 1 tsp black pepper (ground)
- 1 tsp dill weed (dried)

DIRECTIONS:

1. Preheat your air fryer to 200°C
2. Take a large bowl and add the olive oil
3. Add the potatoes, bacon, salt, pepper, dill, and paprika into the bowl and toss to evenly coat
4. Pour the contents of the bowl into the air fryer and cook for 12-16 minutes
5. After 10 minutes, give everything a good stir and continue to stir every few minutes

Perfect Breakfast Bacon

Serves - 2
Calories - 91, protein - 2g, fat - 8g, carbs - 5g

INGREDIENTS:

♦ 4-5 rashers of lean bacon,
fat cut off

DIRECTIONS:

1. Line your air fryer basket with parchment paper, to soak up excess grease
2. Arrange your bacon in the basket, ensuring you don't overcrowd; around 4-5 slices should be enough, depending upon the size of your machine
3. Set the fryer to 200°C
4. Cook for 10 minutes for crispy, and an extra 2 if you want it super-crispy
5. Serve and enjoy!

Patatas Bravas

Serves - 4
Calories - 97, protein - 1g, fat - 4g, carbs - 15g

INGREDIENTS:

- 300g potatoes, cut into chunks
- 1 tbsp avocado oil
- 1 tsp garlic powder
- Pinch of salt
- Pinch of pepper
- 1 tbsp smoked paprika

DIRECTIONS:

1. Bring a large saucepan of water to the boil and add the potatoes, cooking for 6 minutes
2. Strain the potatoes and place them on a piece of kitchen towel, once a little cool, pat dry
3. Leave the potatoes to arrive at room temperate
4. Take a large mixing bowl and add the garlic powder, salt, and pepper and add the avocado oil, mixing together
5. Add the potatoes to the bowl and coat liberally
6. Place the potatoes into the basket and arrange them with space in-between
7. Set your fryer to 200°C
8. Cook the potatoes for 15 minutes, giving them a shake at the halfway point
9. Remove and serve

Pancakes, German Style

Serves - 5
Calories - 139, protein - 8g, fat - 4g, carbs -18g

INGREDIENTS:

- 3 eggs
- 1 cup flour
- 1 cup milk

- Pinch of salt
- 2 tbsp apple sauce, unsweetened

DIRECTIONS:

1. Set your fryer to 200°C and insert a ramekin inside to heat up
2. Place all your ingredients inside a blender and blitz to combine
3. Spray the ramekin with a little cooking spray
4. Pour the batter into the tray or ramekin
5. Fry for between 6-8 minutes, depending on your preference
6. Remove and serve with your favourite toppings!

Loaded Hash Browns

Serves - 4
Calories - 246, protein - 6g, fat - 3g, carbs - 42g

INGREDIENTS:

- 3 potatoes
- 1 green pepper, chopped
- 1 red pepper, chopped
- 1 small onion, chopped
- 2 cloves of garlic, chopped
- 1 tsp paprika
- 2 tsp olive oil
- Pinch of salt
- Pinch of pepper

DIRECTIONS:

1. Grate the potatoes and squeeze out the excess water
2. Place your potatoes in a large bowl of cold water and soak for 25 minutes
3. Drain the potatoes again and pat them dry
4. Transfer the potatoes into a large bowl and add the spices and oil, combining everything together
5. Place your potatoes into your fryer basket and set to 200ºC, cooking for 10 minutes
6. Open the lid and give the potatoes a good shake
7. Add the peppers and onions and cook for another 10 minutes
8. Allow to cool and serve!

Easy Air Fryer Sausage

Serves - 5

Calories - 260, protein - 14g, fat - 21g, carbs - 3g

INGREDIENTS:

♦ 5 links of sausages, uncooked

DIRECTIONS:

1. Line the basket of your fryer with parchment paper
2. Arrange the sausages inside the basket with a little space between them
3. Set to 180°C and cook for 15 minutes
4. Turn the sausages over and cook for another 5 minutes
5. Remove and cool before serving

Grilled Bacon and Cheese

Serves - 2

Calories - 486, protein - 25g, fat - 26g, carbs - 25g

INGREDIENTS:

- 4 slices of regular bread
- 1 tbsp butter
- 2 slices cheddar cheese
- 5 slices of bacon, cooked to your liking
- 2 slices of mozzarella

DIRECTIONS:

1. Melt the butter in the microwave or on the hob
2. Take the bread and spread the melted butter onto one side of each
3. Place one slice of bread into the fryer basket, with the buttered side facing downwards
4. Place the cheddar on top, followed by the bacon, mozzarella and the other slice of bread, with the buttered side facing upwards
5. Set your fryer to 170ºC and cook the sandwich for 4 minutes
6. Turn the sandwich over and cook for another 3 minutes
7. Serve whilst hot and repeat with the remaining sandwich

Easy Omelette

Serves - 1
Calories - 220, protein - 12.9g, fat - 3.5g, carbs - 15g

INGREDIENTS:

- 2 eggs
- 150ml milk
- Pinch of salt
- 40g shredded cheese
- Any toppings you like, such as mushrooms, peppers, onions, etc

DIRECTIONS:

1. In a medium mixing jug, combine the eggs and milk
2. Add the salt and garnishes and combine well
3. Take a 6x3" pan and grease well, before pouring the mixture inside
4. Arrange the pan inside the air fryer basket
5. Cook at 170ºC for 10 minutes
6. At the halfway point, sprinkle the cheese on top and loosen the edges with a spatula
7. Remove and enjoy!

Egg & Ham Cups

Serves - 4

Calories - 82.1, protein - 7.1g, fat - 5.2g, carbs -17g

INGREDIENTS:

- 4 eggs
- 8 slices of bread, pre-toasted
- 2 slices of ham
- A pinch of salt
- A pinch of pepper
- A little extra butter for greasing

DIRECTIONS:

1. Take 4 ramekins and brush them with butter to grease inside
2. Take the slices of bread and flatten them down with a rolling pin
3. Arrange the toast inside the ramekins, rolling it around the sides, with 2 slices in each ramekin
4. Line the inside of each ramekin with a slice of ham
5. Crack one egg into each ramekin
6. Season with a little salt and pepper
7. Place the ramekins into the air fryer and cook at 160°C for 15 minutes
8. Remove from the fryer and wait to cool just slightly
9. Remove from the ramekins and serve

Potato & Chorizo Frittata

Serves - 2

Calories - 421, protein - 27g, fat - 26g, carbs - 17g

INGREDIENTS:

- 3 eggs
- 1 chorizo sausage, sliced
- 1 cubed potato, half boiled
- 40g sweetcorn, frozen works best
- A little olive oil
- Half a small pack of feta cheese
- A pinch of salt

DIRECTIONS:

1. Add a little olive oil to the frying basket
2. Add the corn, potato, and sliced chorizo to the basket
3. Cook at 180ºC until the sausage is browned
4. In a small bowl, beat together the eggs with a little seasoning
5. Pour the eggs into the pan
6. Crumble the feta on top
7. Cook for 5 minutes
8. Remove and serve in slices

Air Fryer Poultry Recipes

Korean Chicken Wings

Serves - 2
Calories - 356, protein - 23g, fat - 26g, carbs - 6g

INGREDIENTS:

- 1kg chicken wings (bones included)
- 1 tsp salt
- 1 tsp ground black pepper
- 2 tbsp gochujang
- 1 tbsp mayonnaise
- 1 tbsp agave nectar
- 1 tbsp sesame oil
- 1 tbsp ginger (minced)
- 1 tbsp garlic (minced)
- 2 packets of Splenda

DIRECTIONS:

1. Preheat the air fryer to 200°C
2. Line a small tin with foil
3. Sprinkle the chicken wings with salt and pepper, place inside the tin and then transfer into the air fryer
4. Cook for 20 minutes, turning halfway
5. Take a medium bowl and combine the remaining ingredients to make the sauce
6. Coat the chicken wings in the sauce, combining well
7. Continue to cook in the air fryer for another 5 minutes

Delicious Tandoori Chicken

Serves - 2
Calories - 178, protein - 25g, fat - 6g, carbs - 2g

INGREDIENTS:

- 500g halved chicken tenders
- 75g Greek yogurt
- 1 tbsp ginger (minced)
- 1 tbsp garlic (minced)
- 1 tsp paprika
- ½ tsp salt
- ½ tsp cayenne
- 1 tsp garam masala
- 1 tsp turmeric
- ½ cup chopped cilantro

DIRECTIONS:

1. Take a large mixing bowl and combine all ingredients, except for the chicken
2. Preheat the air fryer to 160ºC
3. Place the chicken in the air fryer and cover with a little oil
4. Cook for 10 minutes turnover then cook for a further 5 minutes
5. Pour the sauce over the top of the chicken and cook for another 5 minutes
6. Serve!

Cheesy Chicken Chimichangas

Serves - 6

Calories - 486, protein - 25g, fat - 26g, carbs - 25g

INGREDIENTS:

- 6 large tortillas
- 2 chicken breasts, cooked and shredded
- 4 tbsp mild salsa
- ¼ tsp black pepper
- 30g refried beans
- 1 jalapeno pepper, chopped
- 1 tsp cumin
- ½ tsp chilli powder
- ¼ tsp salt

DIRECTIONS:

1. Take a large mixing bowl and combine all ingredients, mixing well
2. Take one tortilla and add a third of the mixture, before rolling up the bottom and the sides to create a burrito
3. Spray the air fryer with cooking spray and heat to 200°C
4. Place the filled wraps into the air fryer and cook for 7 minutes
5. Serve whilst hot

Chicken Jalfrezi

Serves - 4

Calories - 247, protein - 23g, fat - 12g, carbs - 9g

INGREDIENTS:

- 500g chicken, no bones, no skin
- 1 onion, chopped
- 2 bell peppers, chopped
- 4 tbsp tomato sauce
- 1 tbsp water
- 2 tbsp olive oil
- 1 tsp salt
- 2 tsp garam masala
- 1 tsp turmeric
- 1 tsp cayenne

DIRECTIONS:

1. Take a large mixing bowl and combine the oil, chicken, onions, pepper, salt, half the garam masala, turmeric, half the cayenne
2. Transfer the mixture to the air fryer and cook at 180ºC for 15 minutes
3. Take a medium mixing bowl (microwave safe) and add the tomato sauce, water salt, the remaining garam masala and cayenne and combine well
4. Cook in the microwave for 1 minute, stir then cook for a further minute
5. Remove the chicken from the air fryer and pour the sauce over the top.
6. Serve with rice whilst still hot

Turkey and Mushroom Burgers

Serves - 2
Calories - 132, protein - 25g, fat - 26g, carbs - 25g

INGREDIENTS:

- 180g mushrooms
- 500g minced turkey
- 1 tsp garlic powder
- 1 tsp onion powder
- ½ tsp salt
- ½ tsp pepper

DIRECTIONS:

1. Take your food processor and add the mushrooms, pulsing into they form a puree. Season and pulse once more
2. Remove from the food processor and tip into a mixing bowl
3. Add the turkey to the bowl and combine well
4. Take a little of the mixture into your hands and shape into burgers. You should be able to make five
5. Spray each burger with a little cooking spray and place in the air fryer
6. Cook at 160ºC for 10 minutes

Crunchy Chicken Tenders

Serves - 4
Calories - 253, protein - 26.2g, fat - 11.4g, carbs - 9.8g

INGREDIENTS:

- 1 egg
- 2 tbsp olive oil
- 50g dry breadcrumbs
- 8 chicken tenders (frozen)

DIRECTIONS:

1. Heat the fryer to 175ºC
2. In a small bowl, beat the egg
3. In another bowl, combine the oil and the breadcrumbs together
4. Take one tender and first dip it into the egg, and then the breadcrumbs
5. Place the tender into the basket of the fryer
6. Repeat with the rest of the tenders, making sure they don't touch
7. Cook for 12 minutes and serve!

Smoky Chicken Breast

Serves - 2

Calories - 432, protein - 79g, fat - 9.5g, carbs - 3.2g

INGREDIENTS:

- 2 chicken breasts, cut into halves
- 2 tsp paprika
- 1 tsp thyme, ground
- 1 tsp cumin
- ½ tsp cayenne
- ½ tsp onion powder
- ½ tsp pepper
- ¼ tsp salt
- 2 tsp olive oil

DIRECTIONS:

1. In a medium sized bowl, combine the spices together
2. Pour the spice mixture onto a plate
3. Take each chicken breast and coat in the spices, pressing down to ensure even distribution
4. Place the chicken to one side for 5 minutes
5. Preheat your air fryer to 180°C
6. Arrange the chicken inside the fryer and cook for 10 minutes
7. Turn the chicken over and cook for another 10 minutes
8. Remove from the fryer and allow to sit for 5 minutes before you serve

Quick Chicken Nuggets

Servings - 4
Calories - 244, protein - 31g, fat - 3.6g, carbs - 25g

INGREDIENTS:

- 500g chicken tenders
- 4 tbsp salad dressing mix
- 2 tbsp plain flour
- 1 egg, beaten
- 50g dry breadcrumbs

DIRECTIONS:

1. Take a large mixing bowl and add the chicken
2. Sprinkle the seasoning over the top and ensure the chicken is evenly coated
3. Allow the chicken to rest for 10 minutes
4. Add the flour into a resealable bag
5. Pour the breadcrumbs onto a medium sized plate
6. Transfer the chicken into the resealable bag and coat with the flour, giving it a good shake
7. Remove the chicken and dip into the egg, and then roll into the breadcrumbs, coating evenly
8. Repeat with the chicken
9. Heat your air fryer to 200°C
10. Arrange the chicken inside the fryer and cook for 4 minutes, before turning over and cooking for another 4 minutes
11. Remove and serve whilst hot

Bacon Wrapped Chicken Thighs

Serves - 4

Calories - 453, fat - 34g, protein - 150g, carbs - 33g

INGREDIENTS:

- 150g butter, softened
- 1 garlic clove, minced
- ¼ tsp thyme (dried)
- ¼ tsp basil (dried)
- A pinch of salt
- A pinch of pepper
- 5 rashers of bacon
- 5 chicken thighs, no skin or bones

DIRECTIONS:

1. Take a mixing bowl and add the softened butter, garlic, thyme, basil, salt and pepper, combining well
2. Place the butter onto cling film and roll up. Place in the refrigerator for 2 hours
3. Open the butter and place one strip of bacon on top to coat a little
4. Place the chicken thighs on top of the bacon
5. Sprinkle a little extra garlic on top
6. Add a little of the butter into the middle of the chicken thigh and tuck the end of the bacon inside the chicken to secure
7. Preheat the air fryer to 180ºC
8. Cook the chicken until white in the middle

Buffalo Chicken Wings

Serves - 4
Calories - 481, fat - 41g, protein - 20g, carbs - 7g

INGREDIENTS:

- 500g chicken wings
- 1 tbsp olive oil
- 1 tsp cayenne pepper
- 150g butter, softened
- 2 tbsp vinegar
- 1 tsp garlic powder

DIRECTIONS:

1. Preheat the air fryer to 180ºC
2. Take a large bowl and add the chicken inside
3. Drizzle the oil over the wings, coating evenly
4. Cook the wings for 25 minutes and then flip the wings and cook for 5 more minutes
5. Take a medium saucepan over a medium heat and add the butter, vinegar, garlic powder and cayenne pepper, combining well
6. Pour the sauce over the wings and flip to coat
7. Serve!

Air Fryer Seafood Dishes

Tilapia Fillets

Serves - 2
Calories - 724, protein - 41g, fat - 59g, carbs - 13g

INGREDIENTS:

- 50g almond flour
- 2 fillets of tilapia fish
- 2 tbsp melted butter
- 1 tsp black pepper
- ½ tsp salt
- 4 tbsp mayonnaise
- A handful of almonds, sliced thinly

DIRECTIONS:

1. Take a mixing bowl and add the almond flour, butter, pepper and salt, combining well
2. Take the fish and spread the mayonnaise on both sides
3. Cover the fillets in the almond flour mix
4. Spread one side of the fish with the sliced almonds
5. Spray the air fryer with a little cooking spray
6. Add the fish into the air fryer and cook at 160°C for 10 minutes

Zesty Fish Fillets

Serves - 2

Calories - 315, protein - 38g, fat - 14g, carbs - 8g

INGREDIENTS:

- 4 fillets of your choice of fish
- 100g breadcrumbs
- 30g dry ranch seasoning
- 2½ tbsp vegetable oil
- 2 eggs, beaten
- Lemon to serve

DIRECTIONS:

1. Preheat the air fryer to 180°C
2. In a medium bowl, add the breadcrumbs and seasoning, combining well
3. Add the oil to the mixture and combine once more
4. Dip the fish into the egg and then coat in the breadcrumb mix
5. Place in the air fryer and cook for 12 minutes
6. Serve with lemon wedges

Peppery Lemon Shrimp

Serves - 2
Calories - 215, protein - 28.9g, fat - 8.6g, carbs - 12.6g

INGREDIENTS:

- 1 tbsp olive oil
- 350g prepared shrimp, uncooked
- Juice of 1 lemon
- 1 tsp pepper
- ¼ tsp paprika
- ¼ tsp garlic powder
- 1 lemon, sliced

DIRECTIONS:

1. Preheat the fryer to 200ºC
2. Take a medium sized mixing bowl and combine the lemon juice, pepper, garlic powder, paprika and the olive oil together
3. Add the shrimp to the bowl and make sure they're well coated
4. Arrange the shrimp into the basket of the fryer
5. Cook for between 6-8 minutes, until firm and pink
6. Serve!

Crunchy Fish

Serves - 4
Calories - 354, protein - 26.9g, fat - 17.7g, carbs - 22.5g

INGREDIENTS:

- 100g breadcrumbs (dry)
- ¼ cup olive oil
- 4 fillets of your favourite fish
- 1 egg, beaten
- 1 lemon, sliced

DIRECTIONS:

1. Heat the fryer to 180ºC
2. In a medium mixing bowl, combine the olive oil and the breadcrumbs
3. Take the fish and first dip it into the egg and then the breadcrumbs, making sure they are evenly coated
4. Arrange the fish into the basket
5. Cook for 12 minutes
6. Remove and serve with lemon slices

Gluten Free Honey and Garlic Shrimp

Serves - 2
Calories - 486, protein - 25g, fat - 26g, carbs - 25g

INGREDIENTS:

- ½ cup of honey
- 450g shrimp, fresh
- ½ cup gluten-free soy sauce
- 2 tbsp tomato ketchup
- 1 packet of stir fry vegetables, frozen
- 1 garlic clove, crushed
- 1 tsp ginger, fresh
- 2 tbsp corn starch

DIRECTIONS:

1. Take medium saucepan and add the honey, soy sauce, garlic, tomato ketchup and ginger, bringing it to a simmer
2. Add the corn starch and stir continually, until the sauce thickens
3. Take the shrimp and coat with the sauce
4. Line the air fryer with foil and add the shrimp and vegetables inside
5. Cook at 180ºC for 10 minutes

Air Fryer Fish Tacos

Servings - 4
Calories - 486, protein - 25g, fat - 26g, carbs - 25g

INGREDIENTS:

- 500g mahi fish, fresh
- 8 small tortillas
- 2 tsp Cajun seasoning
- 4 tbsp sour cream
- 2 tbsp mayo
- ¼ tbsp cayenne
- 2 tbsp pepper sauce
- A little salt and pepper
- 1 tbsp sriracha sauce
- 2 tbsp lime juice

DIRECTIONS:

1. Cut the fish into slices and season with salt
2. Mix the cayenne pepper and black pepper with the Cajun seasoning. Sprinkle onto fish
3. Brush pepper sauce on both sides of the fish
4. Set air fryer to 180ºC and cook for 10 mins
5. Take a medium bowl and combine the mayonnaise, sour cream, lime juice, sriracha and cayenne pepper
6. Assemble tacos the tacos and serve!

Baked Crunchy Cod

Serves - 5
Calories - 340, protein - 14g, fat - 26g, carbs - 23g

INGREDIENTS:

- 2 pieces of cod cut into smaller portions (around five)
- 4 tbsp of panko breadcrumbs
- 1 egg
- 1 egg white

- ½ tsp onion powder
- ½ tsp garlic salt
- A pinch of pepper
- ½ tsp mixed herbs

DIRECTIONS:

1. Heat air fryer to 220ºC
2. Take a small bowl and mix the egg and then add the egg white and combine once more
3. Cover the top of the fish with the herb mixture
4. Dip each piece of fish into the egg and then cover in the panko breadcrumbs
5. Line air fryer basket with tin foil
6. Place the fish in air fryer and cook for about 15 minutes

Shrimp with Yum Yum Sauce

Serves - 4
Calories - 486, protein - 25g, fat - 34g, carbs - 25g

INGREDIENTS:

- 500g jumbo shrimp, peeled
- 1 tbsp soy sauce
- 1 tbsp garlic paste
- 1 tbsp ginger paste
- ¾ cup mayonnaise
- ¼ cup tomato ketchup
- 1 tsp paprika
- 1 tbsp sugar
- 1 tsp garlic powder

DIRECTIONS:

1. Take a mixing bowl and add the soy sauce, garlic paste and ginger paste, combining well
2. Add the shrimp to the bowl and leave to marinate for 15 minutes
3. In another bowl, add the ketchup, mayonnaise, sugar, paprika and the garlic powder and combine to make the sauce
4. Set the air fryer to 200ºC
5. Place the shrimp in the basket and cook for 8-10 minutes
6. Once cooked, add the sauce and combine

Cajun-Style Shrimps

Serves - 6
Calories - 340, protein - 30g, fat - 26g, carbs - 22g

INGREDIENTS:

- 250g shrimp, cooked
- 14 slices of smoked sausage
- 4 cups part-boiled potatoes, halved
- 2 corn on the cobs, cut into smaller pieces
- 1 onion, diced
- 2 tbsp bay seasoning

DIRECTIONS:

1. Combine all the ingredients in a bowl and mix well
2. Line the air fryer with foil
3. Place half the mix into the air fryer and cook at 200°C for about 6 minutes
4. Combine everything again and cook for a further 6 minutes
5. Repeat for the second batch
6. Serve!

Sriracha with Salmon

Serves - 2
Calories - 320, protein - 25g, fat - 34g, carbs - 25g

INGREDIENTS:

- 3 tbsp sriracha
- 4 tbsp honey
- 1 tbsp soy sauce
- 500g salmon fillets

DIRECTIONS:

1. Take a medium bowl and add the honey, soy sauce and sriracha, combining well
2. Place the salmon into the sauce skin, with the skin facing upwards
3. Allow to marinade for 30 minutes
4. Spray the air fryer basket with cooking spray
5. Heat the air fryer to 200ºC
6. Place the salmon into the air fryer skin side down and cook for 12 minutes
7. Serve!

Air Fryer Beef Dishes

Beef Wellington

Serves - 4

Calories - 400, protein - 20g, fat - 26g, carbs - 19g

INGREDIENTS:

- 1kg beef fillet (one large piece)
- Chicken pate
- 2 sheets of shortcrust pastry
- 1 egg, beaten
- Salt
- Pepper

DIRECTIONS:

1. Season the beef with salt and pepper and wrap tightly in cling film
2. Place the beef in the refrigerator for at least one hour
3. Roll out the pastry and brush the edges with the beaten egg
4. Spread the pate over the pastry, making sure it is distributed equally
5. Take the beef out of the refrigerator and remove the cling film
6. Place the beef in the middle of the pastry
7. Wrap the pastry around the meat and seal the edges with a fork
8. Place in the air fryer and cook at 160°C for 35 minutes

Bulgogi Beef Burgers

Serves - 4
Calories - 392, protein - 24g, fat - 29g, carbs - 7g

INGREDIENTS:

- 500g minced beef
- 2 tbsp gochujang
- 1 tbsp soy
- 2 tsp garlic, minced
- 2 tsp ginger, minced
- 1 onion, chopped
- 1 tbsp olive oil
- 2 tsp sugar

DIRECTIONS:

1. Take a large mixing bowl and add all the ingredients (except the meat), combining well
2. Place the bowl into the refrigerator for 30 minutes
3. Divide the beef into four equal sections and create burgers
4. Place in the air fryer and cook at 180ºC for about 10 minutes
5. Serve in burger buns with the mixture over the top

Sticky Asian Beef

Serves - 2
Calories - 396, protein - 19g, fat - 26g, carbs - 28g

INGREDIENTS:

- 1 tbsp coconut oil
- 500g steak, sliced thinly
- ½ tbsp garlic, minced
- 2 green peppers, sliced
- ½ cup liquid aminos
- ½ cup water
- ¾ cup brown sugar
- ¼ tsp pepper
- ½ tsp ginger, ground
- 1 tsp red pepper flakes
- Pinch of salt

DIRECTIONS:

1. Take a medium saucepan and melt the coconut oil. Once melted, add the peppers and cook until soft
2. In another pan add the aminos, ginger, red pepper flakes, brown sugar, and garlic, combining well. Allow to boil and then turn down to a simmer for 10 minutes
3. Season the steak with salt and pepper and place in the air fryer. Cook at 200ºC for 10 minutes
4. Turn the steak and cook for a further 5 minutes, until crispy
5. Add the steak to the peppers then mix with the sauce
6. Serve with rice

Beef Stir-fry

Servings - 2
Calories - 359, protein - 25g, fat - 32g, carbs - 18g

INGREDIENTS:

- 500g steak
- 500g broccoli
- 3 peppers, cut into strips
- 1 tbsp ground ginger
- ¼ cup water
- 1 onion, sliced
- ¼ cup hoisin sauce
- 1 tsp sesame oil
- 2 tsp garlic minced
- 1 tbsp soy sauce

DIRECTIONS:

1. Take a large bowl and add the sesame oil, hoisin sauce, garlic, soy and water, combining well
2. Add the steak to the bowel and allow to marinate for 20 minutes
3. Mix 1 tbsp of oil with the vegetables
4. Place the vegetables into the air fryer and cook at 200°C for about 5 minutes
5. Place the vegetables in a bowl and place to one side
6. Add the meat to the air fryer and cook for 4 minutes
7. Turn and cook for a further 2 minutes
8. Mix the steak with the vegetables and serve with rice

Beef Fried Rice

Serves - 2
Calories - 250, protein - 19g, fat - 26g, carbs - 36g

INGREDIENTS:

- 100g cooked rice
- 500g beef strips, cooked
- 1 tbsp sesame oil
- 1 onion, diced
- 1 egg

- 2 tsp garlic powder
- 1 tbsp vegetable oil
- 100g frozen peas
- Salt
- Pepper

DIRECTIONS:

1. Preheat air fryer to 175°C
2. Season the beef with salt, pepper and garlic powder
3. Cook the beef in a pan until almost done
4. Mix the rice with peas, carrots and vegetable oil, combining well
5. Add the rice mixture to the beef and combine
6. Add to the air fryer and cook for about 10 minutes
7. Add the egg and cook until the egg has completely cooked

Beef Satay

Serves - 2
Calories - 394, protein - 45g, fat - 26g, carbs - 32g

INGREDIENTS:

- 500g steak, cut into strips
- 2 tbsp olive oil
- 1 tbsp fish sauce
- 1 tsp sriracha sauce
- A handful of cilantro, sliced
- 1 tsp ground coriander
- 1 tbsp soy sauce
- 1 tbsp ginger, minced
- 1 tbsp garlic, minced
- 1 tbsp sugar
- 50g roasted peanuts

DIRECTIONS:

1. Take a large mixing bowl and add the oil, fish sauce, soy, ginger, garlic, sugar sriracha, coriander and half the cilantro, combining well
2. Add the steak and marinate for 30 minutes
3. Add the steak to the air fryer and cook at 200ºC for about 8 minutes
4. Place the steak on a plate and top with remaining cilantro and chopped peanuts
5. Serve with peanut sauce

Beef Kebobs

Serves - 4
Calories - 250, protein - 23g, fat - 15g, carbs - 4g

INGREDIENTS:

- 500g beef, cubed
- 200g low fat sour cream
- 2 tbsp soy sauce
- 1 bell pepper
- ½ onion, chopped
- 8 x 6" skewers

DIRECTIONS:

1. Take a medium bowl and combine the sour cream and soy sauce
2. Add the cubed beef and marinate for at least 30 minutes
3. Cut the pepper and onion into 1 inch pieces
4. Soak the skewers in warm water for about 10 minutes
5. Place the beef, bell peppers and onion onto the skewers, alternating between each one
6. Cook in the air fryer at 200°C for 10 minutes, turn them over at the halfway point

Classic Air Fryer Hamburgers

Serves - 4
Calories - 294, protein - 25g, fat - 26g, carbs - 19g

INGREDIENTS:

- ◆ 500g minced beef
- ◆ Salt
- ◆ Pepper

DIRECTIONS:

1. Preheat air fryer to 200ºC
2. Divide minced beef into 4 equal portions and form them into burgers with your hands
3. Season with salt and pepper to your taste
4. Place in the air fryer and cook for 10 minutes
5. Turn the burgers over and cook for a further 3 minutes

Cheesy Beef Enchiladas

Serves - 4
Calories - 320, protein - 25g, fat - 43g, carbs - 25g

INGREDIENTS:

- 500g minced beef
- 1 packet taco seasoning
- 8 medium tortillas
- 150g grated cheese
- 100g soured cream
- 1 can of black beans
- 1 can of tomatoes, chopped
- 1 can of chillies, chopped
- 1 can red enchilada sauce
- A handful of cilantro, chopped

DIRECTIONS:

1. In a medium frying pan, brown the beef and add the taco seasoning, combining well
2. Add the beef, beans, tomatoes and chillies to the tortillas, spreading equally
3. Line the air fryer with foil and place the tortillas inside
4. Pour the enchilada sauce over the top and sprinkle with cheese
5. Cook at 200ºC for five minutes
6. Remove from the air fryer, add toppings and serve

Chinese Chilli Beef

Serves - 2
Calories - 320, protein - 25g, fat - 34g, carbs - 21g

INGREDIENTS:

- 500g steak, cut into strips
- 4 tbsp light soy sauce
- 1 tsp honey
- 3 tbsp tomato ketchup
- 1 tsp Chinese five spice
- 1 tbsp olive oil
- 6 tbsp sweet chilli sauce
- 1 tbsp lemon juice
- 2 tbsp corn flour

DIRECTIONS:

1. Place the steak into a large bowl and sprinkle over the cornflour and five spice
2. Add to the air fryer and cook for 6 minutes at 200°C
3. Meanwhile, combine the remaining ingredients
4. Add to the air fryer and cook for another 3 minutes
5. Serve!

Air Fryer Mongolian Beef

Serves - 4

Calories - 485, protein - 25g, fat - 26g, carbs - 32g

INGREDIENTS:

- 500g steak, cut into strips
- 100g corn starch
- 2 tsp vegetable oil
- ½ tsp ginger, minced
- 1 tbsp garlic, minced
- 4 tbsp soy sauce
- 3 tbsp water
- 75g brown sugar

DIRECTIONS:

1. Coat the steak with the corn starch
2. Place the steak into the air fryer and cook at 200ºC for 10 minutes, turning halfway
3. Place remaining ingredients in a saucepan and gently warm
4. When cooked, place the steak in a bowl and pour the sauce over the top

Air Fryer Pork & Lamb Dishes

Honey and Mustard Meatballs

Serves - 4
Calories - 357, protein - 22g, fat - 27g, carbs - 7g

INGREDIENTS:

- 500g minced pork
- 1 red onion, chopped
- 1 tsp mustard
- 2 tsp honey
- 1 tsp garlic puree
- 1 tsp pork seasoning
- Salt
- Pepper

DIRECTIONS:

1. Take a large mixing bowl and combine all ingredients well
2. Form into meatballs using your hands
3. Place in the air fryer and cook at 180ºC for 10 minutes

BBQ Ribs

Serves - 2
Calories - 329, protein - 28g, fat - 26g, carbs - 21g

INGREDIENTS:

- 500g ribs
- 3 garlic cloves, chopped
- 4 tbsp BBQ sauce
- 1 tbsp honey
- ½ tsp five spice
- 1 tsp sesame oil
- 1 tsp salt
- 1 tsp black pepper
- 1 tsp soy sauce

DIRECTIONS:

1. Chop the ribs into small pieces and place them into a bowl
2. Add all the ingredients into the bowl and mix well
3. Marinate for 4 hours
4. Preheat the air fryer to 180ºC
5. Place the ribs into the air fryer and cook for 15 minutes
6. Coat the ribs in honey and cook for a further 15 minutes
7. Serve whilst still warm

Pork Belly with Crackling

Serves - 4
Calories - 384, protein - 25g, fat - 23g, carbs - 28g

INGREDIENTS:

- 800g belly pork
- 1 tsp sea salt
- 1 tsp garlic salt
- 2 tsp five spice
- 1 tsp rosemary
- 1 tsp pepper
- 1 tsp sugar
- Half a lemon

DIRECTIONS:

1. Cut lines into the meat portion of the pork
2. Cook thoroughly in water until tender
3. Allow to air dry for 3 hours
4. Score the skin and prick holes into it with a fork
5. Rub with the dry rub mix
6. Also rub some lemon juice on the skin
7. Place in the air fryer and cook at 160ºC for 30 minutes
8. Then cook at 180ºC for a further 30 minutes

Pork Schnitzel

Serves - 2
Calories - 467, protein - 18g, fat - 32g, carbs - 27g

INGREDIENTS:

- 3 pork steaks, cubed
- Salt and pepper
- 75g plain flour
- 2 eggs
- 125g breadcrumbs

DIRECTIONS:

1. Sprinkle the pork with salt and pepper
2. Coat the pork in the flour then dip into the egg
3. Coat the pork in breadcrumbs
4. Place in the air fryer and cook at 175ºC for 20 minutes, turning halfway
5. Serve whilst still warm

Mustard Glazed Pork

Serves - 4

Calories - 422, protein - 29g, fat - 26g, carbs - 39g

INGREDIENTS:

- 750g pork tenderloin
- 1 tbsp minced garlic
- ¼ tsp salt
- Pinch of cracked black pepper
- 3 tbsp mustard
- 3 tbsp brown sugar
- 1 tsp Italian seasoning
- 1 tsp rosemary

DIRECTIONS:

1. Cut slits into the pork and place the minced garlic into the slits
2. Season with the salt and pepper
3. Take a mixing bowl and add the remaining ingredients, combining well
4. Rub the mix over the pork and allow to marinate for 2 hours
5. Place in the air fryer and cook at 200ºC for 20 minutes

Lamb Burgers

Serves - 4
Calories - 423, protein - 30g, fat - 38g, carbs - 3g

INGREDIENTS:

- 600g minced lamb
- 2 tsp garlic puree
- 1 tsp harissa paste
- 2 tbsp Moroccan spice
- Salt
- Pepper

DIRECTIONS:

1. Place all the ingredients in a bowl and mix well
2. Form into burgers, using your hands
3. Place in the air fryer and cook at 180°C for 18 minutes

Tasty Pork Burgers

Serves - 4

Calories - 491, protein - 22g, fat - 30g, carbs - 31g

INGREDIENTS:

- 400g minced pork
- 4 wholemeal burger buns
- A little avocado sauce
- 1 avocado
- 1 onion, chopped
- 2 tbsp spring onion, chopped
- 2 tbsp Worcester sauce
- 2 tbsp tomato ketchup
- 1 tsp garlic puree
- 1 tsp mixed herbs
- Salad to garnish as you like

DIRECTIONS:

1. Take a large mixing bowl and combine the mince, onion, half the avocado and all of the seasonings
2. Form into burgers using your hands
3. Place in the air fryer and cook at 180°C for 8 minutes
4. When cooked, place the burgers into the buns, layer with sauce and add salad garnish

Italian Meatballs

Serves - 12
Calories - 122, protein - 10g, fat - 8g, carbs - 0g

INGREDIENTS:

- 2 tbsp olive oil
- 2 tbsp shallot, minced
- 3 cloves garlic, minced
- ½ cup panko crumbs
- ¼ cup parsley, chopped
- 1 tbsp rosemary, chopped
- 30ml milk
- 300g turkey sausage
- 350g minced beef
- 1 egg, beaten
- 1 tbsp Dijon mustard
- 1 tbsp thyme, finely chopped

DIRECTIONS:

1. Preheat air fryer to 200°C
2. Heat the oil in a pan and cook the garlic and shallot over a medium heat for 1-2 minutes
3. Mix the panko and milk in a bowl and allow to stand for 5 minutes
4. Add all the ingredients to the panko mix and combine well
5. Shape into 1 ½ inch meatballs and cook for 12 minutes

Pork Chops with Healthy Sprouts

Servings - 2
Calories - 337, protein - 40g, fat - 11g, carbs - 21g

INGREDIENTS:

- 250g pork chops
- 1 tsp olive oil
- Pinch of salt
- ½ tsp pepper
- 170g brussels sprouts, quartered
- 1 tsp maple syrup
- 1 tsp Dijon mustard

DIRECTIONS:

1. Season the pork chops with salt and pepper
2. Take a medium bowl and combine the oil, maple syrup and mustard
3. Add the brussels sprouts and combine
4. Add the pork chops and brussels sprouts to the air fryer and cook at 200ºC for about 10 minutes

Breaded Pork Chops

Serves - 6
Calories - 378, protein - 33g, fat - 13g, carbs - 8g

INGREDIENTS:

- 6 boneless pork chops
- Pinch of salt
- 1 egg, beaten
- 3 tbsp panko crumbs
- 2 tbsp crushed cornflakes
- Black pepper

- 2 tbsp parmesan cheese
- 1 ¼ tsp paprika
- ½ tsp garlic powder
- ½ tsp onion powder
- ¼ tsp chilli powder

DIRECTIONS:

1. Heat the air fryer to 200°C
2. Season the pork chops with salt
3. Mix the panko, cornflakes, salt, parmesan, garlic powder, onion powder, paprika, chilli powder and pepper in a bowl
4. Beat the egg in another bowl
5. Dip the pork in the egg and then coat with panko mix
6. Place in the air fryer and cook for about 12 minutes turning halfway

Pork Chops with Honey

Serves - 6

Calories - 486, protein - 21g, fat - 26g, carbs - 19g

INGREDIENTS:

- ♦ 2 ⅔ tbsp honey
- ♦ 1/2 cup ketchup
- ♦ 6 pork chops
- ♦ 2 garlic cloves
- ♦ 2 slices of mozzarella cheese

DIRECTIONS:

1. Preheat air fryer to 200°C
2. Mix all the ingredients together in a bowl, except for the chops
3. Add the pork chops and allow to marinate for at least 1 hour
4. Place in the air fryer and cook for about 12 minutes, turning at halfway

Air Fryer Vegetarian Dishes

Radish Hash Browns

Serves - 4
Calories - 486, protein - 25g, fat - 26g, carbs - 25g

INGREDIENTS:

- 250g radish
- 1 onion, chopped
- 1 tsp onion powder
- ¾ tsp sea salt
- ½ tsp paprika
- ¼ tsp black pepper
- 1 tsp coconut oil

DIRECTIONS:

1. Wash the radishes, trim off the roots and slice in a processor
2. Add the onions and process in the machine
3. Add the coconut oil and mix well
4. Add the onions and radish into the air fryer and cook at 180ºC for 8 minutes, shaking a few times
5. Add the onion and radish into a bowl, season and combine well
6. Transfer everything back into the air fryer and cook at 200ºC for 5 minutes

Falafel Burgers

Serves - 2

Calories - 709, protein - 30g, fat - 26g, carbs - 92g

INGREDIENTS:

- 400g can chickpeas
- 1 small onion, chopped
- 1 lemon
- 140g oats
- 28g cheese
- 28g feta
- Salt and pepper
- 2 tbsp Greek yogurt
- 4 tbsp soft cheese
- 1 tbsp garlic puree
- 1 tbsp coriander
- 1 tbsp oregano
- 1 tbsp parsley, chopped

DIRECTIONS:

1. Take a blender and add the chickpeas, onion, lemon rind, garlic and seasonings. Blend until coarse
2. Add the mixture to a bowl and stir in half the soft cheese, cheese and feta
3. Form into burger shapes and coat in the oats
4. Place in the air fryer and cook at 180ºC for 8 minutes
5. To make the sauce, mix the remaining soft cheese, Greek yogurt and lemon juice in a bowl
6. Once the burgers are cooked, serve with the sauce on top

Lentil Burgers

Serves - 4
Calories - 509, protein - 21g, fat - 8g, carbs - 90g

INGREDIENTS:

- 100g black buluga lentils
- 1 carrot, grated
- 1 onion, diced
- 100g white cabbage, chopped
- 300g oats
- 1 tbsp garlic puree
- 1 tsp cumin
- Salt
- Pepper

DIRECTIONS:

1. Blend the oats until they resemble flour
2. Take a saucepan and add the lentils. Add some water and cook for 45 minutes
3. Steam the vegetables for 5 minutes, until softened
4. Add all the ingredients into a bowl and mix well to combine
5. Form into burgers using your hands
6. Place into the air fryer and cook at 180ºC for 30 minutes

Zucchini Burgers

Serves - 4
Calories - 36, protein - 3g, fat - 1g, carbs - 6g

INGREDIENTS:

- 1 zucchini
- 1 small can chickpeas, drained
- 3 spring onions, chopped
- A pinch of dried garlic
- Salt

- Pepper
- 3 tbsp coriander
- 1 tsp chilli powder
- 1 tsp mixed spice
- 1 tsp cumin

DIRECTIONS:

1. Take a large bowl and grate the zucchini, draining the excess water
2. Add the spring onions, chickpeas, zucchini and seasoning, combining well
3. Bind the ingredients together and form into burgers with your hands
4. Place in the air fryer and cook for 12 minutes at 200ºC

Zucchini Meatballs

Serves - 4
Calories - 203, protein - 9g, fat - 6g, carbs - 29g

INGREDIENTS:

- 150g oats
- 40g feta, crumbled
- 1 egg, beaten
- Salt and pepper
- 150g zucchini

- 1 tsp lemon rind
- 6 basil leaves, sliced thinly
- 1 tsp dill
- 1 tsp oregano

DIRECTIONS:

1. Preheat the air fryer to 200°C
2. Grate the zucchini into a bowl, squeezing any excess water out
3. Add all the remaining ingredients, apart from the oats, and mix well
4. Place the oats into a blender and pulse until they resemble breadcrumbs
5. Add the oats to the bowl and combine everything together
6. Form into balls and place in the air fryer
7. Cook for 10 minutes

Mushroom Pasta

Serves - 4
Calories - 402, protein - 12g, fat - 35g, carbs - 10g

INGREDIENTS:

- 100g mushrooms, sliced
- 1 onion, chopped
- 2 tsp garlic, minced
- 1 tsp salt
- ½ tsp red pepper flakes
- 75g cream
- 45g mascarpone
- 1 tsp thyme, dried
- 1 tsp pepper
- 50g parmesan, grated
- Cooked pasta

DIRECTIONS:

1. Place all the ingredients into a bowl and combine well
2. Heat the air fryer to 175°C
3. Grease a 7x3 inch pan and pour in the mixture
4. Place in the air fryer and cook for 15 minutes, stirring halfway through
5. Pour over cooked pasta and sprinkle with parmesan

Tofu Buddha Bowls

Serves - 4
Calories - 552, protein - 25g, fat - 26g, carbs - 25g

INGREDIENTS:

- 1 block of tofu, cubed
- 3 tbsp soy sauce
- 2 tbsp sesame oil
- 1 tsp garlic powder
- ½ onion, chopped
- Tahini dressing
- 3 punch bay bok choy, chopped
- 600g quinoa
- 1 cumber, sliced
- 1 carrot, shredded
- 1 avocado, sliced

DIRECTIONS:

1. Mix the soy sauce, 1 tbsp sesame oil and garlic powder in a bowl
2. Add the tofu marinade for 10 minutes
3. Place in the air fryer and cook at 200ºC for 20 minutes, turning halfway
4. Heat the remaining sesame oil in a pan and cook the onions for about 4 minutes
5. Add the bok choy and cook for another 4 minutes
6. Divide the quinoa between bowls, add bok choy, carrot, cucumber and avocado
7. Top with the tofu and drizzle with Tahini

Jackfruit Taquitos

Serves - 2

Calories - 326, protein - 25g, fat - 26g, carbs - 18g

INGREDIENTS:

- 500g Jackfruit
- 500g red beans
- 250g pico de gallo sauce
- ¼ cup water
- 4 wheat tortillas

DIRECTIONS:

1. Place the jackfruit, red beans, sauce and water in a saucepan
2. Bring to the boil and simmer for 25 minutes
3. Preheat the air fryer to 185°C
4. Mash the jackfruit mixture
5. Add ¼ of the mix to each tortilla and roll up tightly
6. Spray with olive oil and place in the air fryer
7. Cook for 8 minutes and serve

Macaroni and Cheese Quiche

Servings - 4
Calories - 191, protein - 10g, fat - 8g, carbs - 18g

INGREDIENTS:

- 8 tbsp macaroni cheese
- 2 sheets shortcrust pastry
- 2 tbsp Greek yogurt
- 2 eggs
- 150ml milk
- 1 tsp garlic puree
- A little grated cheese to serve

DIRECTIONS:

1. Rub the inside of 4 ramekins with flour
2. Line the ramekins with the pastry
3. Mix the yogurt, garlic and macaroni together in a bowl
4. Add the mixture into the ramekins, until ¾ full
5. Mix the egg and milk together and pour over the macaroni, before sprinkling with cheese
6. Heat the air fryer to 180ºC and cook for 20 minutes, until golden brown

Potato Gratin

Servings - 4
Calories - 232, protein - 9g, fat - 15g, carbs - 16g

INGREDIENTS:

- 2 large potatoes
- 2 eggs, beaten
- 100ml coconut cream
- 1 tbsp plain flour
- 50g grated cheddar cheese

DIRECTIONS:

1. Slice the potatoes into thin slices and place in the air fryer
2. Cook for 10 minutes at 180°C
3. In a large bowl, mix the eggs, coconut cream and flour together
4. Line four ramekins with the potato slices
5. Cover with the cream mixture and sprinkle with cheese
6. Cook for 10 minutes at 200°C

BONUS!
Air Fryer Side Dishes

Stuffed Jackets

Serves - 4

Calories - 256, protein - 25g, fat - 23g, carbs - 32g

INGREDIENTS:

- 2 large baking potatoes, russets work well
- 2 tsp olive oil
- 150g yoghurt
- 120ml milk
- ¼ tsp pepper
- A handful of spinach, chopped
- 2 tbsp yeast
- ½ tsp salt

DIRECTIONS:

1. Preheat the air fryer to 190ºC
2. Rub the potatoes with oil to coat completely
3. Place the potatoes in the air fryer and cook for 30 minutes
4. Turn the potatoes and cook for a further 30 minutes
5. Cut each potato in half and scoop out the centre
6. Mash with the yoghurt, milk and yeast, until well combined
7. Stir in the spinach and season with salt and pepper
8. Add the mixture back into the potato skins and place in the air fryer
9. Cook at 160ºC for about 5 mins

Grilled Bacon & Cheese

Serves - 2
Calories - 389, protein - 22g, fat - 26g, carbs - 29g

INGREDIENTS:

- 4 slices of white bread
- 1 tbsp butter
- 2 slices of cheddar cheese
- 2 slices of mozzarella
- 5 slices of pre-cooked bacon

DIRECTIONS:

1. Melt the butter either over the hob or in the microwave
2. Spread the butter onto one side of the bread
3. Place one slice of bread into the fryer basket, with the buttered side facing down
4. Place the cheddar on top, followed by the bacon, mozzarella and the other slice of bread, with the buttered side facing upwards
5. Set your fryer to 170ºC and cook the sandwich for 4 minutes
6. Turn the sandwich over and cook for another 3 minutes
7. Turn the sandwich out and serve whilst hot
8. Repeat with the other remaining sandwich

Avocado Fries

Serves - 2
Calories - 319, protein - 9.3g, fat - 18g, carbs - 39.8g

INGREDIENTS:

- 75g white flour
- 1 tsp water
- ½ tsp black pepper
- ¼ tsp salt
- 1 peeled avocado, cut into 8 pieces
- 1 egg, beaten
- 75g panko crumbs

DIRECTIONS:

1. Preheat the air fryer to 200°C
2. Take a small bowl and combine the flour salt, and pepper
3. Mix the egg and water together in another small bowl and add a third of the breadcrumbs
4. Dip the avocado into the flour, then the egg, and then into the breadcrumbs
5. Spray with cooking oil and place in the air fryer
6. Cook for 4 minutes
7. Turn and cook for a further 3 minutes

Simple Fries

Serves - 2
Calories - 97, protein - 2.3g, fat - 1.2g, carbs - 19.8g

INGREDIENTS:

- 3 large potatoes cut into chips, around ½" in size
- 1 tsp olive oil
- ¼ tsp salt
- ¼ tsp pepper

DIRECTIONS:

1. Place the potatoes in a bowl and cover with water, soaking for 30 minutes
2. Pat the potatoes dry with kitchen paper
3. Drizzle with oil and toss to coat
4. Place in the air fryer and cook at 200°C for about 15 minutes, keep tossing through the cooking time
5. Sprinkle with salt and pepper before serving

Garlic & Parsley Potatoes

Serves - 4
Calories - 89, protein - 2.4g, fat - 0.1g, carbs - 20.1g

INGREDIENTS:

- 500g baby potatoes, quartered
- 1 tbsp oil
- 1 tsp salt
- ½ tsp garlic powder
- ½ tsp dried parsley

DIRECTIONS:

1. Preheat the air fryer to 175ºC
2. Combine potatoes and oil in a bowl and combine well
3. Add remaining ingredients and mix together, combining everything once more
4. Transfer to the air fryer and cook for about 25 minutes until golden brown, turning halfway through

Stuffed potatoes

Serves - 4
Calories - 288, protein - 9.3g, fat - 10.3g, carbs - 40.1g

INGREDIENTS:

- 4 baking potatoes, peeled and cut into halves
- 1 tbsp olive oil
- ½ cup grated cheese
- ½ onion, diced
- 2 slices of uncooked bacon

DIRECTIONS:

1. Preheat air fryer to 175ºC
2. Brush the potatoes with oil and cook in the air fryer for 10 minutes
3. Coat again with oil and cook for a further 10 minutes
4. Cut the potatoes in half and spoon the insides into a bowl, reserving the skins to one side
5. Add the cheese and combine
6. Take a medium frying pan and cook the bacon and onion in a pan until brown
7. Add the potato to the pan and combine
8. Stuff the skins with the mixture and return to the air fryer
9. Cook for about 6 minutes

Easy Potato Wedges

Servings - 4
Calories - 120, protein - 2.5g, fat - 5.3g, carbs - 19g

INGREDIENTS:

- ◆ 2 potatoes with skins on, cut into wedges
- ◆ 1 ½ tbsp olive oil
- ◆ ½ tsp paprika
- ◆ ⅛ tsp ground black pepper
- ◆ ½ tsp parsley
- ◆ ½ tsp chilli powder
- ◆ ½ tsp salt

DIRECTIONS:

1. Preheat the air fryer to 200ºC
2. Add all ingredients to a bowl and combine well
3. Place the wedges into the air fryer and cook for 10 minutes
4. Turn and cook for a further 8 minutes until golden brown

Citrus Infused Tofu

Serves - 4
Calories - 109, protein - 8g, fat - 9g, carbs - 11g

INGREDIENTS:

- 500g tofu, drained
- 1 tbsp tamari
- 1 tbsp corn starch
- ¼ tsp pepper flakes
- 1 tsp minced ginger
- 1 tsp fresh garlic

- 1 tsp orange zest
- 3 tbsp orange juice
- 100ml water
- 2 tsp corn starch
- 1 tbsp maple syrup

DIRECTIONS:

1. Cut the tofu into cubes, place in a bowl
2. Add the tamari and combing well
3. Mix in half of the corn starch and allow to marinate for 30 minutes
4. Take another bowl and combine the rest of the ingredients
5. Place the tofu in the air fryer and cook at 190ºC for about 10 minutes
6. Take a large saucepan and add the tofu, combining with the sauce
7. Cook until sauce thickens and serve

Asparagus Fries

Serves - 2
Calories - 188, protein - 0.6g, fat - 2.3g, carbs - 9g

INGREDIENTS:

- 1 egg
- 12 asparagus spears, prepared
- 1 tsp honey
- 75g panko breadcrumbs
- Pinch of cayenne pepper
- 75g parmesan, grated
- 50g mustard
- 4 tbsp Greek yogurt

DIRECTIONS:

1. Preheat air fryer to 200°C
2. Take a medium bowl and combine the egg and honey
3. Take a medium plate and pour the panko crumbs and parmesan on top
4. Coat each asparagus in egg, and then in the breadcrumbs
5. Place in the air fryer and cook for about 6 mins
6. Mix the remaining ingredients in a bowl and serve as a dipping sauce

Celery Root Fries

Serves - 2
Calories - 168, protein - 1.8g, fat - 12.9g, carbs - 13g

INGREDIENTS:

- ½ celeriac, cut into pieces
- 600ml water
- 1 tbsp lime juice
- 1 tbsp olive oil
- 50g mayonnaise
- 1 tbsp mustard
- 1 tbsp horseradish, powdered

DIRECTIONS:

1. Take a large bowl and add the celeriac
2. Add the water and lime juice, and soak for 30 minutes
3. Preheat air fryer to 200ºC
4. Take another bowl and combine the mayonnaise, horseradish and mustard. Place in the refrigerator
5. Drain the celeriac and drizzle with oil. Season with salt and pepper
6. Place in the air fryer and cook for about 10 minutes, turning halfway
7. Serve with the mayonnaise mixture as a dip

BONUS!
Air Fryer Desserts

Amber C. Gardner

Tempting Chocolate Cake

Serves - 4
Calories - 573, protein - 41g, fat - 134g, carbs - 253g

INGREDIENTS:

- 3 eggs
- 75g sour cream
- 220g flour
- 150g sugar
- 2 tsp vanilla essence
- 220g butter
- 50g cocoa powder
- 1 tsp baking powder
- ½ tsp baking soda

DIRECTIONS:

1. Preheat the air fryer to 160°C
2. Take a large mixing bowl and combine all ingredients
3. Grease a baking tin and transfer the mixture to the tin
4. Place into the air fryer
5. Cook for 25 minutes and decorate with your favourite topping

Tangy Apple Pie

Serves - 2
Calories - 395, protein - 15g, fat - 32g, carbs - 25g

INGREDIENTS:

- 1 packet of ready to roll pastry
- Cooking spray
- 1 large apple, chopped
- 2 tbsp lemon juice
- 1 tbsp cinnamon
- 2 tbsp sugar
- ½ tsp vanilla essence
- 1 tbsp butter
- 1 egg, beaten

DIRECTIONS:

1. Preheat the air fryer to 200°C
2. Take a baking tin and cut a piece of pastry about ½ inch bigger than the tin
3. Take another piece of the pastry, a little smaller than the tin
4. Spray the tin with cooking spray and place the larger piece of pastry inside
5. Take a large mixing bowl and combine the apple, cinnamon, sugar, lemon juice and vanilla
6. Pour the mix into the tin and top with butter
7. Place the other piece of pastry on top and pinch around the edges
8. Pierce a couple of slits in the top
9. Brush with the egg
10. Cook in the air fryer at 160°C for 30 minutes

Shortbread Cookies

Serves - 2
Calories - 385, protein - 18g, fat - 32g, carbs - 24g

INGREDIENTS:

- 250g flour
- 75g sugar
- 175g butter
- 1 tbsp vanilla essence
- Chocolate buttons for decorating

DIRECTIONS:

1. Preheat air fryer to 180°C
2. Take a large bowl and combine all ingredients, apart from the chocolate, and rub together
3. Form a dough and roll out to around 1cm thick
4. Cut the dough with your favourite cookie cutter
5. Place in the air fryer and cook for 10 minutes
6. Place the chocolate buttons onto the shortbread and cook for another 10 minutes at 160°C

Chocolate Lava Cakes

Serves - 4
Calories - 385, protein - 22g, fat - 26g, carbs - 22g

INGREDIENTS:

- 1 ½ tbsp self raising flour
- 3 ½ tbsp sugar
- 75g butter
- 75g dark chocolate, chopped
- 2 eggs

DIRECTIONS:

1. Preheat the air fryer to 175°C
2. Grease 4 ramekin dishes
3. Melt the chocolate and butter in the microwave for about 3 minutes
4. Take a small bowl and combine the eggs and sugar with a whisk, until pale
5. Pour the melted chocolate into the mixture and combine carefully
6. Fold in the flour
7. Fill the ramekins, leaving around an inch at the top
8. Place into the air fryer and cook for 10 minutes

Nutella & Banana Sandwich

Serves - 2

Calories - 376, protein - 14g, fat - 32g, carbs - 19g

INGREDIENTS:

- A little softened butter for spreading
- 100g chocolate spread
- 4 slices of regular white bread
- 1 ripe banana

DIRECTIONS:

1. Preheat air fryer to 175°C
2. Spread the butter on one side of the bread
3. Spread the chocolate spread on the other side
4. Slice the banana into pieces
5. Arrange the banana on top of the chocolate spread
6. Place another slice of bread on top with the chocolate side down
7. Cut the sandwiches into 2 triangles
8. Place in the air fryer and cook for 5 minutes
9. Turn and cook for a further 2 minutes

Peachy Pies

Serves - 8
Calories - 486, protein - 25g, fat - 26g, carbs - 25g

INGREDIENTS:

- 2 peaches, peeled and chopped
- 1 tbsp lemon juice
- 3 tbsp sugar
- 1 tsp vanilla extract
- ¼ tsp salt
- 1 tsp corn starch
- 1 pack of ready to roll pastry

DIRECTIONS:

1. Take a large bowl and combine the peaches, lemon juice, sugar and vanilla
2. Leave to stand for 15 minutes
3. Drain the peaches, keeping 1 tbsp of the liquid to one side
4. Mix corn starch into the peaches until well combined
5. Cut the pastry into 8 circles, and fill with the peach mix
6. Brush the edges of the pastry with water and fold over to form half moons
7. Crimp the edges to seal
8. Coat with cooking spray
9. Add to the air fryer and cook at 170°C for 12 minutes, until golden brown

Apple Chips with Yogurt Dip

Serves - 4
Calories - 104, protein - 1g, fat - 3g, carbs -17g

INGREDIENTS:

- 1 apple
- 1 tsp cinnamon
- 2 tsp oil
- 3 tbsp Greek yogurt
- 1 tbsp almond butter
- 1 tsp honey

DIRECTIONS:

1. Thinly slice the apple and place in a bowl
2. Coat the apple with cinnamon and oil
3. Coat the air fryer with cooking spray and add the apple slices
4. Cook the slices for 12 minutes at 180°C
5. Take a small bowl and combine the butter, honey and yogurt
6. Serve with the apple slices as a dip

Imitation Pop Tarts

Serves - 6
Calories - 229, protein - 2g, fat - 9g, carbs - 39g

INGREDIENTS:

- 150g strawberries, quartered
- 75g sugar
- ½ pack ready to roll shortcrust pastry
- 50g icing sugar
- 1 ½ tsp lemon juice
- 1 tbsp sprinkles

DIRECTIONS:

1. Take a medium bowl and combine the strawberries and sugar
2. Allow to stand for 15 minutes and then microwave on high for 10 minutes, stirring halfway through
3. Roll out pie crust into a 12" circle and then cut into 12 rectangles
4. Spoon the mixture onto six of the rectangles
5. Brush the edges with water and top with the remaining rectangles
6. Press around the edges with a fork to seal
7. Place in the air fryer and cook at 175°C for about 10 minutes
8. Mix together powdered sugar and decorate add sprinkles

Cinnamon Donuts

Serves - 9
Calories - 399, protein - 15g, fat - 32g, carbs - 28g

INGREDIENTS:

- 75g sugar
- 2 ½ tbsp butter
- 2 egg yolks
- 500g flour
- 2 tbsp butter, melted
- 1 ½ tsp baking powder
- 1 tsp salt
- 50g sour cream
- 1 tsp cinnamon

DIRECTIONS:

1. Take a large mixing bowl and combine half the sugar and butter (non-melted) together, using a fork
2. Add the egg yolks and combine
3. Take another bowl and sift the flour, salt and baking powder
4. Add half the sour cream and a third of the flour mix to the butter and combine
5. Mix in the remaining flour and sour cream, before placing in the refrigerator
6. In a small bowl, combine the rest of the sugar and cinnamon together
7. Roll out the dough to ½ inch thick and cut out 9 circles
8. Cut a small circle out of the centre of each
9. Preheat the air fryer to 175°C
10. Brush the donuts with half of the melted butter
11. Place in the air fryer and cook for 8 minutes
12. Brush with the remaining butter and sprinkle with cinnamon mix

Banana Cake

Serves - 4
Calories - 347, protein - 5.2g, fat - 11.8g, carbs - 5.6g

INGREDIENTS:

- 50g brown sugar
- ½ tbsp butter
- 1 banana, mashed
- 1 egg
- 2 tbsp honey
- 220g self raising flour
- ½ tsp cinnamon
- A pinch of salt

DIRECTIONS:

1. Preheat the air fryer to 160°C
2. Spray a small tube tray with cooking spray
3. Take a mixing bowl and beat the sugar and butter together until creamy
4. Take another bowl and combine the banana, egg and honey
5. Mix into the butter until smooth
6. Sift in the remaining ingredients and mix well
7. Spoon into the tray and cook in the air fryer for 30 minutes

CONCLUSION

And there you have it! Many truly delicious air fryer recipes which show you just how easy this piece of machinery is to use.

Whether you opt for a quick, tasty breakfast, or you go all out and impress your guests with your meat dishes, air fryers are a fantastic addition to your kitchen. Not only will you be able to create lower calorie dishes, therefore improving the health of those dining with you, but you'll also be able to achieve that perfect crisp - without added sogginess!

Try as many of these recipes as you can and when you become a little more confident with your air fryer and the way to use it, don't be afraid to tweak them a little and add the extras that you enjoy. The great thing about the air fryer is that it is so flexible, and there are very few foods and ingredients that don't work with it.

Which is your favourite? You'll be hard picked to choose just one from the huge number we've just shown you!

Enjoy!

DISCLAIMER

This book contains opinions and ideas of the author and is meant to teach the reader informative and helpful knowledge while due care should be taken by the user in the application of the information provided. The instructions and strategies are possibly not right for every reader and there is no guarantee that they work for everyone. Using this book and implementing the information/recipes therein contained is explicitly your own responsibility and risk. This work with all its contents, does not guarantee correctness, completion, quality or correctness of the provided information. Misinformation or misprints cannot be completely eliminated.

Printed in Great Britain
by Amazon